From the

Heart of Dixie

DIXIE QUALLS

authorHOUSE®

AuthorHouse™
1663 Liberty Drive
Bloomington, IN 47403
www.authorhouse.com
Phone: 1 (800) 839-8640

Published by AuthorHouse 09/16/2016

ISBN: 978-1-5246-2366-1 (sc)
ISBN: 978-1-5246-2365-4 (e)

Library of Congress Control Number: 2016912898

Print information available on the last page.

Dedication

I want to thank:

God for the many blessings he has given me and the opportunities that he has placed in my path.

My parents for teaching me that you can do anything you set your mind to if you just try.

My friends, especially Jeff and Nikki, and my cousin Bryan who have always been there to give me a push and keep me inspired when I thought writing was a crazy idea.

I want to thank my children, Alex and Hollie, who are the best parts of me, for their unconditional love and support. I want them to know how important it is to always reach for the stars! Put your mind to it and anything is possible.

Come Sit With Me

Come sit with me
In my swing,
Enjoy the view
And a drink.
Come and rest
Your weary head,
In a place
Where you can think.

Come sit a spell
dream a dream,
Make a wish, or say a prayer.
Come spin a tale
Think your thoughts
And enjoy the fresh air.

Come share my swing
Enjoy the breeze
Let the sun beam on your face.
Come sit under
The Maple trees
In this very special place.

Death Comes In Its' Own Time

It is a crisp fall morning and you can feel the electricity in the air. The power that surrounds us, the life force that is ever present. Yes, I am in my swing and my companion, Cookie Eloise, is sniffing away, once again on the trail of a new adventure.

Speaking of life force, being a nurse has provided me with MANY personal and professional relationships that I cherish; Being a hospice nurse has to be one of the hardest, most rewarding, yet emotional jobs I have ever had; second ONLY to being a mother.

Death is not something I fear. I don't want to die, not quite yet, but I know when I'm gone I will be kept alive in the hearts of those who have known me. A quote, that I love, from Ernest Hemingway says, "Every man's life ends the same way. It is only the details of how he lived and how he died that distinguish one man from another."

Over the past 25 years I have taken are of many patients, not just hospice I have tried to give them each the best I could give. I have taken care of my family members as well as friends throughout the years, including those who were hospice or hospice appropriate. I try to explain early on, the difference in quality of life versus quantity and that it is quite selfish to expect your loved one to endure an intolerable existence. This discussion is never easy. Death itself is NEVER easy. It is ALWAYS emotional. I have learned to suppress those emotions and allow myself the opportunity to release the flood of feelings when I am in my own personal space. That doesn't mean I am emotionless with my patients and families, but I am there to impart support and comfort for them, not them for me.

With time, the catastrophic pain of death eases. We, the living, recover and devise new ways to move forward, to live with the loss. That doesn't mean you miss the loved one any less, but you learn to deal with the loss and live with the wonderful memories.

Death comes when it is meant to come. Sometimes it cuts a life short. Death is an absolute. It is an obligation we all have and one that is unavoidable. You only get one chance at this life, one chance to live life to the fullest before you hit that expiration date. Don't live your life for how others feel it should be lived. Allow yourself the power to follow your heart and listen to your inner voice.

Peace, Love, and Blessings!

Decisions

Wow! It has been a day, not a lot of swing time this evening but I have enjoyed the alone time today and have had a lot of time to think about so many different things. Sebastian Pole penned that,"As we embrace our passions and delve into the mystery of life, we unite with the majestic complexity of nature; and if we follow the signs, this can help us understand who we really are."

In this life I have been met with consternation, as well as, hopes and dreams that have yet to be found. I am learning to believe in myself, trust my heart, recognize those opportunities and desires that have been missed out on, and recognize my strength and personal wisdom.

I find myself frequently in thought overload. The business making it hard to concentrate. The psychological baggage weighing me down. What I am finding is that the inviting change and thinking of the possibility that once we let go of the life we know, makes it easier to see the future. I am not afraid of my journey. I am not afraid of being knocked down on my journey, for suffering is a necessary evil in attaining any goal.

Believe in yourself and know that you CAN succeed. Find a purpose in life and set yourself free. Let go and move on from the past. Focus on those things which you can change. Be patient and wait for what you deserve. Those are the things that will enhance your life, your future. Let go of those who bring you down. Learn to appreciate that liberation.

Don't deny your past but know that it has made you who you are today, interesting, original and unique. You can only be you. You cannot be what everyone wants you to be. I guess what I am trying to say is, on my journey to find myself and accept myself, the hardest thing has been to realize that everyone isn't going to like or appreciate me, or my decisions. Once I accepted this, my journey because much less complicated.

Peace, Love, and Blessings!

Depression

Swing time this evening with my Cookie Eloise has been very uneventful. She was being a funny dog running and playing, and I was exhausted from the days duties.

Loved looking at the beauty around me today. The area we live in is rich in beauty and history. They sky today went from a glorious blue to partly cloudy and the sunset was stunningly orange, pink, purple, and gray. The storm clouds are moving in and the temperature is dropping.

This time of year people seem to suffer more from depression. Depression is a wound that cannot be seen. These wounds are more intense and poisonous than anything that you can see outwardly. Depression is insidious. It is an invisible agony. It alienates and tortures one's soul. The blackness, hopelessness and loneliness that a person feels is not easily concealed. There is no cure. You can only learn how to care for these wounds and constantly attempt to keep them away.

To do this you must have patience. Find the courage to be excited with whatever it is that comes your way. Don't always expect the worse. Remember that, "Every man has his secret sorrows which the world knows not; and often times we call a man cold when he is only sad." Henry Wadsworth Longfellow

Peace, Love, Blessings!

Disappointment, Don't let it bring you down

It's a muggy night but I'm sitting in my swing, doing my thing. Thinking about how we, as humans, treat each other and the disappointment: that abounds. There is no doubt how much I love my family and friends. They all know I am a phone call away if they need me for anything, and I frequently ask if they need me to help them with anything. That is who I am. I will always do my best for them, because that is what you do for those you care about.

You see, what I thought I had learned was that you can give too much of yourself. When this happens, eventually, there isn't anything left for you to give. Then people seem to no longer give two cents about you. But I realized, to truly care about someone is an amazing kind of freedom. It allows you to truly feel alive. It is one of the most authentic and compassionate feelings. It gives you the confidence to approach life with vengeance. It gives you the strength and the integrity you need to succeed.

Sometimes, the way things happen, people don't give themselves enough credit, so perceiving one's own self worth can be very difficult. It is important to see yourself as a bright and shining light in this universe. When you can do this, the feeling is one of intense satisfaction.

Well, basically, it doesn't matter how educated you are or how much money you have, you will face disappointments in this life. These disappointments are inevitable but they will strengthen you. This strength will intensify your self confidence. Do not let disappointment bring you down. There is always something good to come from even the worst case scenario, you just have to look.

Peace, Love, and Blessings!

Don't Hesitate

It is a beautiful evening to be sitting outside and Cookie Eloise is laying at my feet. She is such a lazy dog today!!

Swing sitting, on the beautiful fall day, has me reflecting on how quickly things can change. People have a tendency to hesitate in life. They wait until it is too late to say the things that were needed to be said, do the things that should have been done, and feel the emotions they are afraid to feel.

We, as human beings, need to remove our blinders. We need to look at what is important in life. Sometimes we even need to venture outside of our comfort zones. Pain is something we cannot escape. Time will heal all wounds. The scars will be there and should be worn proudly to show how far we have come, instead of being ashamed of them and hiding them.

No one person's life is more perfect than another person's life. We all have regrets, struggles, and have made mistakes. Some of us have made more than others. The key is to not spend time trying to change the but to learn from them and move forward. Desiring what never was is normal. Longing for what never was and what might have been is a waste of time and energy. It brings about nothing but dissatisfaction.

Pick yourself up. Keep moving forward. I don't want to be weighed down. "Make a rule of life never to regret and never to look back. Regret is an appalling waste of energy; you can't build on it; it is only good for wallowing in." Katherine Mansfield

Peace, Love, and Blessings!

Don't Miss Out on Today

Sitting here in my swing, enjoying the morning, and thinking about life. We all know that life is what you make of it. Some of our decisions are good and some are bad, but no matter what, you have to keep your head held high and keep your eyes on the future. It takes a lot of courage to take your life by the horns and live it! Life is not made of coincidences, so never take anything for granted. Life is grand and should be lived in that fashion. It is not always perfect, nor is it a fairy tale, but it is the ups and downs that make life beautiful and make us who we are supposed to become in this life.

Don't miss out on life by worrying about yesterday, which you can't change, or tomorrow, which you can't keep from coming. When you worry about something, it steals away the happiness you could experience today, at this very moment, worrying doesn't help you prevent what may or may not happen tomorrow. Don't complicate your life with worry. Live your life every day. Don't compare your life with someone else's, because you only see what others want you to see anyway. You see their 'highlight reel', not their reality. If you think about it, your 'highlight reel' is probably pretty fantastic as well!

What I am rambling about is this...Don't miss out on today! Life doesn't come with a guarantee that it will always be great, but it does guarantee that everyone's life, in its own way, will be extraordinary. Embrace it! Love it! Live it!

Peace, Love, and Blessings!

Simple is Good

It has been a beautiful Fall day; one of reflection, homework, paperwork and some quality time outside with Cookie Eloise, and the grand dog Dozer.

So many times we lose track of what, or who, is really important to us in this life. It seems that we are so interested in everything else, the important things take a backseat. Yes, I am as guilty as anyone, but I am hoping that realizing that it is a problem will help me to rectify the situation with myself.

Those who are important to me may, or may not, hear from me daily, or even weekly, but they are always in my thoughts. We get so busy with work, school, and basically life, that we don't take the time- let me rephrase, we don't make the time to reach out to those who are important to us. It is the people in our lives, not our possessions, that are important. Visit, text, message, or call just to say "hi" can make such a difference in someone's life. Don't ever take something that simple for granted.

Peace, Love, and Blessings!

Expectations

Well, it's a chilly night for swing sitting. Have so much on my mind and can't figure out how to turn my mind off.

Those great expectations one has, the perception of how things should be, how you want them to be, is nothing more than your wish. Wishes for things to be different, wishes to be prettier, thinner, richer, happier, wishes that things would turn out differently. But the truth is, things turn out just the way they should, the way God planned.

We don't have to like it, we don't have to understand it, we just have to accept what we are given in this life and learn from the bad, revel in the good. It is important that we learn the lessons placed before us and keep surviving this life.

Many tears will flow, happy and sad, much laughter will be shared, and words will be said. Some of these words will be said out of anger and some out of love. This is part of it, they are what molds us, our personality and our lives. Expect nothing. Make the best of what you have. Be thankful for the small things.

Peace, Love, and Blessings!

Family Is All We Have

Well, it is a nippy 61 degrees outside this morning. I am sitting here in my swing listening to the birds chirping and watching Cookie Eloise continuing to walk back to the porch as if to say, "let's go back inside, it's cold." Needless to say, she is stuck out here with me for a while.

I have found, in the last few years, the significance of family. Growing up, I had cousins at my house all the time. On my mom's side, her brother, my Uncle, and his family would come visit almost every week. On my dad's side, his sisters and brothers that lived close, and his nieces and nephews came to visit quite often as well. I grew up as the youngest 'grandchild' on both sides of the family, and with that said, I grew up with a LOT of cousins! I have some first cousins that are about my dad's age, so I grew up with their kids.

My children have not benefited from the luxury of growing up with a lot of their cousins, knowing a lot of my family, or getting to spend time with them. Over the past few years, I have reconnected with aunts, uncles, cousins, and I am so blessed to have had them in my life and I have missed them so much! I have also met even more distant relatives and cannot imagine my life without them being a part of it.

What I have found is that family is where we begin and where we end. Family is about overcoming the past and moving into the future. It is everything! It is a network of those who have helped you to become the person you are. The love of family is something that cannot be substituted with something else. It is distinctive and very unique.

My family is definitely not your typical family. After many years and lack of communication, when I needed them, I didn't have to ask for a thing. They were with me, showing me love and support and letting me know they were there for me, unconditionally. For better or worse, we are family. It has been an awesome experience! I just hate the time we lost and I promise that won't happen again.

I so love my family and getting to talk with them and spend time with them more than they could ever imagine! What I want, is for everyone to know that life isn't always going to be easy. We aren't always going to see eye to eye with our family. In the end, family is all we have, and to ignore that bond and not acknowledge its' importance, in my opinion, foolish! Go spend some time with your family.

Peace, Love, and Blessings!

Always Look for the Positive

Oh my goodness what a beautiful morning to be sitting outside in my swing. Cookie Eloise just loves being outside, especially on these beautiful, sunny, cool mornings; with dew on the grass, the birds singing, and on occasion the beautiful, lonesome sound of a train's whistle. Enjoy the peace and beauty of this day!

Today is one of those days that is going to go down in the history books. It is the 141st Kentucky Derby! There is always something new and exciting going on in life and you really don't have to look very hard to find it. What's really exciting for me is having the opportunity to spend some time with my children, even though they are grown. I cannot tell you how proud I am of them and how excited I am for them at this time in their lives. There are so many opportunities available out of there for them.

Life is good here at my house. Thanks be to God for all his many blessing. Enjoy this day with your friends and or family. Take advantage of the time you have with them. Always look for the positive.

Peace, Love, and Blessings!

Family

Wow! It has been a beautiful, crisp, Autumn day and I've spent a lot of time in my swing. The best swing time today was spent sharing my swing with my cousin while Cookie Eloise was sitting listening to us laugh!

Some of my best times are spent in my swing and I love sharing that time with my cousin. As I have mentioned before, family is very important to me. I will take every opportunity to spend time with them.

Life is a gift. Prioritize. Know what is important. Family is more important than wealth. Family is our inspiration, our driving force.

Troubles come and go. Family is there to support and protect you. Family should have your back. Everything isn't ways going to be perfect. Your family isn't always going to agree with you but they should ALWAYS love you and when the rest of the world is against you. Family should always be there without question.

I want my family to know how much I love them and how special they all are to me, especially some of my cousins who have always been there for me.

"Other things may change us, but we start and end with family." Anthony Brandt

Peace, Love, and Blessings!

Games as a Kid

Finally home! Too pretty of an evening not to get some swing time in and Cookie Eloise is sniffing her way through the yard.

I remember days like this when I was growing up. The sky is so blue it looks as if you could see right through it. The sun is blazing down at an angle shading the glorious mountain keeping the leaves from burning another day. The breeze is faint, yet the day is cool with mild humidity, making even the saddest person smile at the days' beauty.

Days like this, as a kid, were spent outside. Once I got home from school. I would ride my bicycle around the neighborhood or several of us would get up a game of kickball in the field across the street. Sometimes we would even play in the street since we lived on a one way street with very little traffic. I remember first base was the water meter in the front of the apartments across the street. Second base was anything we could find to lay in the road and third base was the Tulip tree in my front yard. Home plate was again, anything we could find to lay down in the road. Sometimes one of us would kick that ball all the way to the end of the street. That never made any of us happy and once that happened the game was over.

Playing Home Free and Tag were other fall activities we enjoyed. We would, of course, play them in Spring and Summer, but it was different in the Fall. The days were crisper, the air was clearer, and of course we had to be inside a bit earlier.

The sun has faded and grown dim. The stars are high in the sky, twinkling and flickering like magic. It is such a unique life we live. Our childhood memories are always with us, some as hazy reflections, other as memories evoked by a certain song, melody, or sound. That is the aching familiarity that makes us wish we were kids again.

Take pleasure in the small things. Experience the joy in what makes you happy. Believe in yourself. Think about your blessings, for your childhood has helped to mold you into the individual you are today. Just look at the beautiful, wonderful, and extraordinary person you have become.

Peace, Love, and Blessings!

Life

What a beautiful Fall morning! The air is crisp, the soft, cool breeze is moving the clouds across the sky and the sun is peeking through, wanting to make its' appearance. Yes, I have been in my swing for quite a while this morning, and Cookie Eloise is sniffing around as well, looking for her own adventure.

It feels really good sitting out here just relaxing and spending time reflecting on my life's journey. I try to live my life and not just exist. This journey is mine. The road has been precarious at times, yet I continue to reach for the stars. There are going to be good things happen and bad things happen along my journey. It is my decision as to whether or not I look for the good or for the bad.

I want to live a bold life. Looking back, it seems I have hesitated and not harnessed the limitless opportunities that have been along that path. That is not saying that the path I chose was good or bad, just that along the way, opportunities may have been missed and they may never come my way again.

You see, life is magic. It is nothing more than an illusion. The future and the past are intertwined to provide us with the present; the opportunity to live the life with which we have been blessed. Focusing on what is ever present, the here and now, is a relatively hard task. If it is taken for granted, it will prevent us from experiencing the limitless opportunities in our lives. I personally don't want to miss a thing.

Peace, Love, and Blessings!

Grow and Learn

One has to sit and contemplate things sometimes. Even when the weather does not permit me to be in my swing, I find the time to think things through. Life has a way of throwing things at you that you would never imagine; good, bad, exciting, and unexplainable. No matter what it is, there is always a silver lining if you look deep enough. Every event helps you to grow and learn.

I have worked the past 20 years in home health and now I work for an insurance company doing in home nurse visits. When the weather gets bad, I will call my clients, on their scheduled days, not just to check on road conditions, but to see if I could make my visit, and to make sure they were ok and see if they needed anything. I generally ask about alternate heat sources, food, medications, things that are a staple for everyone. When I do this, they are all very quick to tell me if they feel I do not need to get out and to make sure I stay safe.

One evening, after a bad snow, I received a couple of messages from clients letting me know their roads were bad. One of them said she would rather me wait until my next scheduled visit than to have me get out and something happen to me. Another said, "be careful if you get out tomorrow, you know how you are. I don't wanna lose my nurse."

If I have ever questioned whether or not I did a good job, or if I had bonded with my clients, the snow this particular season definitely proved to me that I do make a difference. I always want to inspire my clients, and they know I'd do what I can to help them.

It is good to know that I do make such a difference in their lives, for Lord knows they do mine!

Peace, Love, and Blessings!

Halloween

I was up early as predicted, but making good use of my time swing sitting, before the rain comes back. Miss Cookie Eloise is out here with me and she is chasing the leaves as they fall to the ground.

The holidays are quickly approaching and the weather is getting cooler each day. I remember growing up in a small town as a small child. I was not fond of Halloween or trick or treating. As I got older, I learned to appreciate the season and had the opportunity to go trick or treating to many of the houses close to mine. My friend and I would walk down the road a couple of blocks and up the hill, which is much smaller now than in my memories, to a house where a little old couple lived, we went to church with, and just couldn't wait for the treat! They always gave out homemade popcorn balls! Oh how I can still taste them!

Back then we didn't have to be so cautious about the candies and goodies we received. People were genuinely good. I remember being about 12 years old the first time I heard anyone mention needing to have an x-ray of candy to look for razor blades or other foreign objects. Even at that age I was dumbfounded. Why would anyone want to hurt a child? I guess some things will never make sense.

It seems as time progresses things in this world just keep getting worse and this holiday gets a bad reputation all the way around. Evolving from the Celtic holiday marking the end of the harvest season and beginning of winter. It was also believed to be a season for the dead to bridge from one world to the next. Now it is more about parties, costumes, and candy.

Well, times are still changing and Halloween is still one of my favorite holidays! The splendor and elegance of the bright colored leaves, the atmosphere coming alive with electricity and the excitement on the faces of the children who look forward to experiencing what it's like to be someone or something else for a couple of hours is priceless. I would hate to see the trick or treating tradition have to stop, like it did during

WW2. Of course, this time it would not be due to a sugar shortage, but in my opinion, due to incomprehensible acts of terror towards children. Again, why hurt a child?

Well, the morning is getting away from me and it looks as though the rain is back. Please be safe this Halloween and enjoy the season!

Peace, Love, and Blessings!

Happy Healthy Adults

Got to spend some time with my baby girl today. She is only 21 years old. We sat in the swing and just chilled while Cookie Eloise ran around carrying sticks.

The time I get to spend with my kids seems to be getting more and more infrequent. Yes, I wanted them to grow up and become happy and healthy adults with good morals and values; but sometimes, I miss the days when they were young and needed their Momma.

They both graduated college while working full time. Boy how the time has flown!

I remember, when living in Georgia, we did little league soccer, FLES competitions (Foreign Language in Elementary Schools) with my son, and gymnastics and soccer with my daughter. Working full time and running both kids sure kept us busy. Then moving back home near family there was cheerleading, football, recreational league/ Upward basketball for both kids (yes my daughter played football). Then there was travel basketball, recreational league volleyball, and piano lessons for my daughter. My son had little league baseball, and guitar lessons. As they got older they participated in school sports every season. Lets not forget about Youth group, 4 H camp, summer church camps and sports camps. Their senior years in high school they both managed to work in a part time job. SHEW! Did I mention they both were in the top 20 of their classes! Maybe we kept them too busy, but they definitely learned what was important, how to manage their time, and prioritize.

No one said being a parent was easy, and if they did, well, they lied! But it IS one of the hardest, most rewarding jobs you will ever have. All it takes is a little understanding, some patience, and a LOT of love. Children are formed from little scraps of wisdom we give them, life's experiences and watching their parents. Making sure I was present and an active part of their lives growing up and allowing them to learn from their mistakes was important to me. Protecting them from disappointment was impossible, but teaching them how to handle it was key and at times challenging.

Children are the greatest gift God will ever give you. I so enjoy the glimpses of the future I see in my children, the wonder that is still in their eyes, and the hope for a new and exciting tomorrow. I hope the love, respect, and confidence my children have is because no matter what, they know that I believe in them and that they are important.

Peace, Love, and Blessings!

He Walks in the Starlight

He walks in the starlight
His silhouette shines
Eyes sparkling with hope
Thoughts circling his mind.

His heart is big
His shoulders are strong
His touch is gentle
To him life's a song.

He wants to open his heart
To feel love and joy
To share hopes and dreams
No one can destroy.

The vulnerability he feels
The transformation he has made
The feelings are inevitable
Never to fade.

Unbreakable, impenetrable, irredeemable some say
His heart of stone
Is slowly melting away.

I Am Who I Am

I have so enjoyed the last few days off work. It has provided me with the opportunity to get a few things taken care of here at the house, as well as getting to spend some extra time in my swing, thinking (of course that's where I am right now!)

See, I have decided that being loyal to oneself is of the utmost importance. I want many things out of life, and I have finally realized that what I want is just as imperative and important as what others want.

I feel my life is full of changes and challenges that are allowing me to grow. I want to feel my own soul. I want everything life has to offer. I want bright and sunny, as well as the cold and dark, for life is always full of surprises.

The mountains have taught me how to look up and rise to the challenge. The ocean has taught me to keep pushing ahead even when I am pulled back. I try to turn struggles into extraordinary moments that will provide purpose and passion not only in my life but in the lives of others. I strive to achieve personal freedom from the restraints life has to offer, for these freedoms must be fought for and protected.

You see, I am much more than what you perceive. My life is full of infinite possibilities, many blessings, and a bright future. If you cannot accept me for who I am, how I look, or my talents, I suggest you move on, for you are not needed in my life. I may not be perfect but I AM real.

Peace, Love, and Blessings!

I Needed You Here

I needed you here
Such a beautiful soul
With a heart of gold
You trans-versed our hold.

That very moment when you were here no more;
Like an eagle your soul did soar,
Away from us, into God's arms
To suffer no more, to be free from all harm.

Why did you leave? Why did you have to go?
So much needed be said,
So much I should have been told.

Life can be hard, not fair,
and full of pain,
But your pain is eased,
and your suffering has waned.

I will miss you, your voice, your touch and your hands,
Your love and hugs when life I barely can stand.

My Mother, best friend and secret keeper,
The one who throughout my life was a constant teacher.

The lessons are vast,
the memories too few
Your unconditional love will always see me through.

I Want to be Me

I want to be me and nothing more. I want to be every single thing it's possible for me to be. Every day contains a new and exciting universe that is full of potential. In my life I want to live life to the fullest. I want to experience everything that I can. I want to love with every piece of my heart and bring all my dreams into existence. I plan to continue to enlighten my life and show that patience and persistence will provide happiness and improved self esteem.

Being wealthy is much more than a monetary quest. Wealth is love, learning, family and freedom, as well as all those little unspecified occurrences or events that make you smile. With all of these, along comes those feelings that are negative and cause chaos in our universe. The combination of all these feelings help us to grow, learn and live.

You see, life is supposed to be lived, not to be miserable and die. It is my goal to do more than merely live life. As William Arthur Ward penned, "Do more than belong: participate. Do more than care: help. Do more than believe: practice. Do more than be fair: be kind. Do more than forgive: forget. Do more than dream: work."

Peace, Love, and Blessings!

Anger

His voice would resonate in anger, I would shake inside and try to stand
tall to his words
His looks contorted as if he was wondering who I was, why I was, and
how dare I question a thing.
His scent entwined with cigarettes and his touch,
His touch no longer passionate for me.

What have I done to cause such a change? What can I do to repair what
is frayed?
Where do we go from here?

He cried tears of joy the day we wed,
He cried tears of happiness with the birth of each child,
As time moved forward
His confidence became frustration
His willingness became withdrawn.

I felt abandoned, alone, vulnerable
I didn't know this man
This was not the sweet, exciting man who I had come to know,
This was a monster with whom I could share nothing.

He would beat his chest like a gorilla, hit the wall or the door,
And through gritted teeth would curse me until I could bear it no more.

Life had become a chore
Not worth living,
But there are children to think of
Although they are small no more.

Tension is part of life
Suppression deadens the soul
Feelings have no meaning
When will life return,
Will life ever again be whole.

The memories remain vivid and agonizing
With the implosion of feelings
Inevitable
How long will I be in this immobilized state?
Why did the tension become fear?

Unbearably, I travel forward
Searching for my freedom,
For the sweet release from these feelings
Ever searching for happiness

I Will Not Break

Try as you might, I will not break, the walls are built too high.
To protect and save myself from feelings, lest I die.

Your words, they cut like a knife,
But I don't feel the pain,
I am numb to all this strife and
I will not take the blame.

You so underestimate,
Listening to the spoken word,
Such a difference in hearing and listening
My speech, it isn't slurred.

You do not listen with intent to understand,
You should listen instead of speak.
Broken may be my heart but I am no longer weak.

Often we underestimate,
the potential of a listening ear,
It's overwhelming to consider
What possible words I may hear.

All being said and done
Your words burnt into my soul
I am now but one
And no longer under your control.

Invisible

Invisible, that may be it,
I'm invisible, so no one can see...
At least not who I really am or who I want to be.

My voice, seems it doesn't make a sound,
I speak, but no one cares...
They hear not what I try to say, only what they want to hear.

I give from my soul
My heart's boundaries are few..
No one understands me, that my feelings are true.

The feelings I experience
No one understands
Feelings I cannot share upon demand.

To understand those feelings
To experience that touch
To know your truly loved for such.

My imperfections have become beauty
My weaknesses are now my strengths
.Learning how it doesn't matter what anyone else thinks.

It is Fall, Time for Self Renewal

Well, Cookie Eloise and I are at it again this morning...swing sitting that is. It is such a beautiful day! The sun is up, allowing us to feel and see its' warmth and magnificence. There is an ever so slight breeze that is keeping us from getting too hot.

Today is the local Labor Day, Celebration. Anyway, sitting here I got to thinking about when I was younger and when the parades first began. There were so many participants, bands, floats, old cars, tractors, and of course the beautiful horses at the end...it seemed as if the parade took a couple of hours, and let's not forget all the vendors that set up and sold their arts and crafts.

The church I belonged to always had a float in the parade. We would work on it a couple of times the week before the parade. The fellowship was wonderful. There was always laughing, music, singing, and talk of how we were destined to win with our float. Ha Ha! Yes, there are still judges and floats still win trophies or plaques.

Some of my best teenage memories were at church. Besides working on the float for the parade, our youth group would go bowling, skiing, hiking. It was awesome! As a parent working with children's church, directing bible school, being active with my kids in Little League and Recreational League as a coach, and taking their youth group on trips and participating with other local youth groups have also been experiences I would never trade and can never forget.

I have met some magnificent people and these experiences have shaped me in ways I cannot explain. You really have to get to know someone to understand them. I don't mean get to know what they allow you to know, because that is sometimes not them at all, but what they want to portray. Really get to know someone; all the good, bad, and indifferent. Bryant McGill said, "The power of getting to know one another is so immense, eclipsed only by first getting to know ourselves." And the scary part, I think, is accepting yourself.

As confusing as it sounds, that is my thought process for today.

Peace, Love, and Blessings!

I've Never Been Free

I've never been free to be me
Never had the chance to see.
My parent's daughter, my husband's wife and children's mother
Three jobs that I have loved and none could be tougher.
But...learning who I am, where I belong,
Am I doing this right or is this all wrong?

I've never been free to be me
Never had the chance to see.
Years of building walls that none could tear down,
To protect and provide solitude from life's deafening quiet sounds.
The walls bear resemblance to days gone by,
Hiding the smiles and laughter with not a reason to cry.
No one knows the pain inside, or the intensity of this thing we call life.

I've never had the chance to be me
Never had the chance to see.
I have a job that I love, yet requires me to feel,
So, I go thru the motions and pretend that they are real.
Emotionless is how I feel inside
To survive this pain that I continue to hide.

I've never had the chance to be me
Never had the chance to see.
Am I good or am I bad?
Is there a chance I could be happy again, not sad.
The flood of emotions I'm afraid I will feel,
How much longer can I stay in this hell?
To be free from worry and free from pain,
To live my life free from these constraints.

I've never had the chance to be me
Never had the chance to see.
God is with me, this I know,
Without his touch I would already be gone.
These feelings are real, although hard to believe
I only allow people to see what I want them to see.
Secrets are a way of life,
I would not want to cause others strife.

I've never had the chance to be me
Never had the chance to see.
My adult years have been painful and heartbreakingly so,
My how life throws you curves
But onward you must go.

Leaves

Sitting in my swing this evening while Cookie Eloise played in the leaves brought back so many memories. When my children were small, they absolutely loved jumping in and playing in the leaf piles. As they got older, it continued to be a fun Fall pastime until they were in their middle teen years. That being said, now I enjoy watching my sweet Cookie Eloise play and roll in the leaves.

Once when I was about 11 years old, I remember having dinner, (the mid day meal), and after eating, my mom and I walked down the road a couple of blocks. I remember it was a chilly yet sunny day with a rather sharp breeze blowing. The rain of the magnificently colored leaves landing on the ground as we walked brought about a definite beauty. Looking back, the time spent with my Momma was even more beautiful. The rain falls, the wind blows, the leaves swirl around, and the colors change. Just as times change, my kids have gotten older and they now help with raking the leaves instead of playing in them, albeit not half as much fun.

The memories are there as is the love we share. My kids are carving out their pumpkins and I could never be prouder.

Peace, Love, and Blessings!

Let Your Family Know You Love Them

Sitting here, all alone, looking out the window at the mountain, with the trees turning green, the dogwoods in bloom and the dark clouds rolling in, I am reflecting on family. I have some family who are truly an inspiration with their faith in God. Never pretend to be someone or something you aren't. Be encouraged to follow your dreams and your heart. Always have a positive spin on everything. You see, being a Christian and having faith is important to me.

Through the years, I lost the closeness with my family that I had growing up. The past few years, I have worked hard to reconnect and stay in contact with my family. The author Rick Riordon penned, "if there's one thing I've learned over the eons, it's that you can't give up on your family, no matter how tempting they make it. It doesn't matter if they hate you, or embarrass you, or simply don't appreciate your genius..." And with that being said, I'm thankful that my family never gave up on me and I am proud of my family, each and every one for they all are special and mean the world to me.

I know I take my family for granted and for that I apologize. We don't know if we will be around for another birthday for tomorrow is not promised. Take each day to let those you love ow that you love them. You can't choose your blood family so just accept them, flaws and all. Love them and respect them for who they are.

Peace, Love, and Blessings!

Life is an Adventure

Sitting out in my swing this morning I was thinking about everything I need to get done. The list continues to grow daily. Work, homework, errands for me and the kids, and let's not forget to stop and smell the coffee (or roses).

I have never been one to procrastinate, and I have always had excellent time management skills. It just seems like the past 10 months have been a little harder. Wow! I just realized something....that is how long I've been back in school. Hahaha! Go figure!

I am thankful for the job I have, the flexibility and support from those I work with. I am thankful for the opportunity to go back to school, and do well! I am thankful for my home, and the fact that one person doesn't make too much of a mess. (That being said, I guess it isn't really that messy.) I am thankful that I have people I can call on when I need them to help me, although I am a little stubborn and don't do it often. I am also VERY thankful for those few people in my personal life whom I can depend on to listen to me fuss, whine, cry, give me support, or a good swift kick in the arse when needed!

They say money is the root of all evil, but when you are in school, at any age, procrastination runs a close second. I tend to either procrastinate a bit or I go into overdrive and work my self into oblivion. Sometimes it is hard to find that happy medium, but with age comes wisdom, and I am learning (such a slow process)!

That being said, I love my life and appreciate those who help make it so special. My circle is small and I hope those who are in that circle know how special they are and how much they are appreciated. Life is an adventure! Live it! Embrace it! Enjoy it! You only get one chance so make it worthwhile!

Peace, Love, and Blessings!

Life is Ever-changing

Life is ever changing
With all its twists and turns
These changes are inevitable
This we must discern.

In every change,
There is some beauty,
In every change,
There is some pain.
Change is like the weather,
Sunshine, snow and rain.

Change is like a flower, blooming in the warm sunshine,
Or like the brilliance of lightning, as it flashes across the sky.
Change is like the beauty of snow, falling and glistening oh so bright,
Or the glorious look of stars as they illuminate the night.

Life with it's ever changing course
Can lead you along the way
Lessons that must be learned
All about love and hate.

Life has its' twists and turns
A journey that helps you to grow
Uncertainties that turn to lessons
That work together to make you whole

Love

So far it's been an odd day filled with lots of different thoughts.

Anyway, this morning while sitting in my swing, watching Cookie Eloise rolling around in the yard, I was thinking about a movie. Love is essential, but I begin thinking about my romantic future and I found inspiration from this movie. You see, I am a die hard romantic. I know we each have our own definitions of what a die hard romantic is, and I guess mine may be a little different from most. To me being a die hard romantic is totally different from being a hopeless romantic. It is a whole approach to life and to love.

You see, there is an art to living. That art involves several things including being sensitive to the beauty of nature and the essence of the human connection. There is an irrepressible joy in experiencing life with another person. Small gestures can be very sentimental. I don't find these things to be negative. I do feel that it is important to awaken your soul. This can be elusive for some.

Without love there is nothing. Believing in love can be very hard. Have faith for it comforts the heart and soul. Allow yourself to be opened up to the amazing feelings you can have when you experience unconditional acceptance. Everyone is deserving of love and affection from someone. It is my hope that we each find that at least once in our lifetime.

1 Corinthians 13:4-8 "4 Love is patient, love is kind. It does not envy, it does not boast, it is not proud. 5 It is not rude, it is not self-seeking, it is not easily angered, it keeps no record of wrongs. 6 Love does not delight in evil but rejoices with the truth. 7 It always protects, always trusts, always hopes, always perseveres. 8 Love never fails..."

Peace, Love, and Blessings!

Be All You Can Be

Got to sit in my swing for a long time today while Cookie Elosie was running around carrying sticks.

I had worked weeding two of four flower beds and picking up some smaller sticks today, and just enjoying my time in the yard. I had my earbuds in with my music playing, and was just enjoying the day. Afterwards, I sat in my swing for a while and got to thinking about what is really important and realized I needed some courage. Courage to take risks, otherwise, I will never achieve those things that are important to me.

I am very much an individual, and I have been learning to love myself and not worry about anyone else's judgement; for they should not be judging me in the first place. Learning to not care what others think has been a struggle for me. It isn't that I don't care about their opinions, but I am learning to respect my own decisions. You see, focusing on my decisions and my goals help to keep me looking ahead. This way I don't keep looking behind me wondering "what if". I have read that there is no amount of guilt that can change the past. That means there is no amount of anxiety that can stop the future.

Strong people haven't had an easy past. They work hard and have been through more than you can realize. Their life has many chapters. You should never compare their journey with yours. It is never too late to be who or what you want to be. The author C. Joybell C. penned that, "The only way that we can live, is if we grow. The only way that we can grow is if we change. The only way we can change is if we learn. The only way we can learn is if we are exposed. And the only way we can become exposed is if we throw ourselves into the open."

We can't be afraid of change or to allow ourselves to change. Stepping onto a new path can be scary and difficult. The one thing I do know is that I must be loyal to myself. This is what will allow me to grow and change.

It is a challenge, but allows me to realize who I am and understand what I think.

Destiny is something to be achieved, not to be waited for. People will try to find a way to crush your dreams, your destiny. Just remember that these people lack the courage and determination to follow their own dreams. They can't see how their negativity affects them much less you, so you have to not let their negativity affect you. Speak it as though it is, believe it and it will happen.

I know you are wondering where all my ramblings are leading so I guess to recap and make it simple...Choose to live life, make positive change, be motivated, be useful and excel. Changes bring opportunities beyond what we can comprehend. Will it be easy? No. Will it be worth it? Yes. Never stop working on becoming the best you can be.

Peace, Love, and Blessings!

March

March proves itself to never be changing,
the feelings they won't go away.
So much I needed to learn and know,
why won't the pain just go?
It's been many years, yet the empty feeling is still here,
Why did you have to go and leave me in despair?
Resentment is how I'm feeling, even after all these years,
you left me questioning life's daily lessons, crying many tears.
Abandoned, devastated, empty is how I still feel when I think of you.
How much I miss you and love you to this day still shines through.

Me and Life

Well, things don't always work out the way you expect, but on this beautiful Fall evening. I am able to enjoy my swing and watch the fading sun to the West as Cookie Eloise rolls in the fallen leaves.

Over the past few years, I have learned not to expect anything from anyone. You see, if you don't expect anything, you are never disappointed. It is a defense mechanism I adopted and it has proven itself very valuable. Now though, I am realizing that trying to be what everyone thought I should be caused me to not know who I really am. I am proud to say I am no longer held captive in that past.

I am a work in progress and have been finding out a lot about myself. What I have found is that I like myself. I still have some hang ups that require some attention; but I truly think some, not all, are not MY problem, but the problem of others, so we will have to see where that leads.

I have accomplishments that I am very proud of and a purpose to my future, as well as having my priorities in order. I don't ask for assistance. I don't ask for guarantees. Just to know that I have begun to listen to my soul and I have learned from my experiences.

Life is an extraordinary gift. It is one we often take for granted. Don't place yourself in a box and place those limits on life. Anything is possible. Regardless of our past experiences, we are all magnificent creatures. We have a spectacular future!!

Peace, Love and Blessings!

Me

Being plagued with my own mortality daily makes me wary at times and seeing enlightenment from many different avenues. I have grown a lot the past few years and have learned that some changes are phenomenally amazing while others are agonizingly challenging. Making conscious choices, speaking honestly, and having the courage to live life to the fullest has, in the past overwhelmed me and left me dismayed but is now beginning to make me feel amused, liberated even.

The intimate relationship between yourself and your soul, getting to now who you are and being inspired daily by those wonderful enough to have been allowed to enter your life, no matter for how long, is something to not take lightly. I work hard to make a living and I have no desire to be faced with regrets in my future. I am building my dreams.

It won't be an easy task, but I hope we can all dream and build our dreams, not tomorrow but begin building today. Take a chance and live the life you have been blessed with. Make the best decisions you can, based on the lessons you have learned. This is your life, the only one you will get, so don't waste it.

Peace, Love, and Blessings!

Mother's Day

Well, I have been outside by myself this morning, in my swing, enjoying the beauty of Mother's Day and just thinking….

It is hard to imagine that my momma has been gone since 1988. I miss her every day but I know she is looking down on me, still loving me, and watching over me. When I think about something I want to tell her, which is practically daily, I go ahead and tell her. No one could ever replace her and no one has ever tried.

When my mom died, my ex-mother in law stepped in and has always been there for me, even to this day! I don't know what I would have ever done without her in my life.

Seven years after my mom died, my dad remarried. She, my step mother, is so good to him and that is all I could ever want. She never tried to replace my mom and has told me how much she respects my mom; for without her, my dad wouldn't be the man she met and fell in love with.

You see, I know these two women love me and are there for me. We may not talk often, and we may not see eye to eye, we may not be blood related…but biology has nothing to do with it.

Happy Mother's Day to all the phenomenal women in the world!

Peace, Love, and Blessings!

My Children

So, I have been doing some thinking about the changes in my life the past few years and I am so amazed and proud of my little family. I have the highest respect for my children and their accomplishments.

My children are polar opposites of each other in many ways, yet they are also very similar. They may not have always taken the road I would have preferred, but it was the road they had to take for themselves. They have embarked on their journey in this life with a determination, a passion, and a vision that leaves me speechless.

Each obstacle seems to be looked upon as a stepping stone for achievement. I envy the opportunities provided them. Neither of them seem to have chosen the easiest path, yet they run from the disorder and chaos in their paths. They are both realists. They have the courage to take the challenges life hands them and turn them into great opportunities.

Learning to let go and allow them to live their own lives, to learn from their own mistakes, and to move forward with their dreams can be a challenge. This challenge is one that is exciting and brings an infinite amount of pride and joy. Knowing that my children are independent, hard working, and will have an education to fall back on helps me to realize that although the future is always lurking close by and is never certain, their future is bright and full of adventure and excitement. I'm thankful for the opportunity to be their mother and I love them better than life itself.

Peace, Love and Blessings!

Not My Problem

It is a cool, somewhat windy Saturday morning. The grass is wet with dew and Cookie Eloise is not wanting to venture off the sidewalk. I have been sitting in my swing thinking, which should not come as a surprise, but maybe I think too much.

I have been doing a LOT of thinking the past few days about how things in life change. We may not always like the changes and may feel they are not always for the better, but either way, those changes are what shapes us and helps us to develop into who we are to become in this life.
Here is a quote that really hit home. "We are never truly loved, until we are loved for WHO and not What we are" Olaotan Fawehinmi

Not everyone is going to like us, like what we do, or how we look. Sometimes people would be surprised if they would just give someone a chance, get to know the person by who they are and not their appearance or the mistakes they have made.

We are not our looks. We are not our mistakes. We are so much more! We are sacred and we are splendid persons that are worthy of respect and acceptance. We are not all equal, but we all are unique. We have to accept ourselves so that others may accept us, as hard as that can be at times.

I know, for myself, I have a good heart. I am a good person. I have made mistakes and wrong decisions. I AM human. Also, I AM intelligent, talented, self sufficient, outspoken, and I am NOT a size 2. I have also learned, apparently, that is called intimidating, which in my book translates into someone is gonna miss out. The other thing I have learned, is the fact that it isn't MY problem. It is their problem.

Peace, Love and Blessings!

Recognize The Good

Good morning! I'm sitting out here in my swing this cool, crisp morning, watching Cookie Eloise roll around in the dew. I am thinking about how blessed I truly am in this life.

Life isn't easy. Life isn't fair. Life isn't perfect. Albert Einstein once said." There are only two ways to live your life. One is as though nothing is a miracle. The other is as though everything is a miracle." One just has to make that conscious choice. This life is what you make it out to be.

Just because you fail once, make one mistake, doesn't mean you are a disaster or that you are going to fail at everything. Keep aspiring for better and hold on, for life is a bumpy ride full of gullies and inclines. Most importantly, always believe in yourself, for if you don't, no one will.

Each and every single day is an open opportunity to live your life to the fullest. You will find tons of blessings and opportunities that are purposely placed, just for you. All you have to to is just open your eyes and look around. Accept them for what they are intended. That doesn't mean you will be free from displeasure, just that every bridge offers a blessing if you are willing to look for it.

Recognize all the good in your life and be thankful for each and every day.

Peace, Love, and Blessings!

Recognize What You Have

Wow! After a busy morning and afternoon with my 'study buddies', I got home and started some laundry, opened a few windows, along with the back door, and I took a nap, which is something I never do. Now I am enjoying some much needed, relaxing, therapeutic swing time with my Cookie Eloise and my grand dog Dozer. They are sniffing around, I think, trying to find the bunny rabbit that is in the field across from the house.

This is a beautiful time of year. A time filled with reflection and thankfulness, not that any other time of year isn't. There are so many things we take for granted in this life and even more that we should be thankful for.

So many times, it seems, we get caught up in what we want and turn a blind eye to the fact that we may actually have what we need. Having what we need is a necessity, but having what we want, well that's just icing on the cake.

When you are thankful for what you have, it is easy to realize just how blessed you really are. Recognize what you have and give thanks for it because there are many who have so much less. Family, friends, good health, a job, groceries....if you thought about it, you would be amazed at the people who don't have these things. There are people in the county in which I live who still have outside bathrooms and minimal running water, yet they are thankful.

Today it is my thought that a thankful heart and inner peace go hand in hand.

Therefore do not be anxious, saying, 'What shall we eat?' or 'What shall we drink?' or 'What shall we wear?' For the Gentiles seek after all these things, and your heavenly Father knows that you need them all.
- Matthew 6:31-32

Peace, Love and Blessings!

Remember Me

Remember me when I am gone
And all the times we have had
For life can be gone in an instant
All feelings from happy to mad.

I leave behind our memories
Don't keep them locked away
Recall them often and with fondness
So with you I will always stay.

But death is matter of fact
Dying on my own terms is how it will be
I want to die with no regrets
Having lived a good life and dying with dignity.

Be Thankful

My goodness, the heat and humidity are horrible, but sitting in my swing always seems to bring me pleasure, even if it is only for a brief period of time. Cookie Eloise and Dozer are inside enjoying the air conditioning and not even wanting to come outside at the moment.

Things don't always work out the way we want them to. That doesn't make it wrong or right, it just makes it what it is. Just breathing, trusting and knowing that the plan God has for us is how it is happening. Everything has a purpose and a time and God's plan includes enough time for everything that's supposed to happen, to happen.

As children learning to walk, we fell many times and had to get back up and try again. As adults we stumble and when this happens, we must regain ourselves and try again. You see, although we have free will to make our own decisions, God has a divine plan and everything we experience is part of that plan. How we deal with our stumbling blocks is the difference in living with stress or living an adventure.

Simple things in life can become complicated, especially when you expect too much from a person or situation. The best thing to do is to survive life with minimal disappointment and be able to experience the glorious plan God has for you.

Be thankful for what you have and for the events that cause you to grow. Learn from your mistakes for they help increase your confidence and help you to grow. No matter how much you survive, good or bad, never let go of those memories, for they are there to remind you from where you came and that even though you cannot change the past, you have the opportunity every day, to create a new ending, a better ending. One thing that will help this process is to always forgive yourself for making mistakes and forgive those who wrong you, but never forget. You see when you forgive, it totally changes your attitude; But if you forget, you tend to lose the knowledge of what you learned.

Peace, Love, and Blessings!

Childhood

What a beautiful morning! The sun is shining, the birds are singing and I have been in my swing for a little while just thinking.

It is funny the things you remember at times, not even understanding why they cropped up in your mind. I recall one time, I was very young, maybe 6 or 7, I had been with my momma to go get her hair fixed at the local beauty shop. I always went with her and it was always fun going there. They would let me play with curlers and look at stuff, yes, that means touching, to my momma's dismay. Anyway, for some reason, this time I didn't get to play. You know if someone new was around you had to be on your best behavior!

After showing my good breeding for so long, I had to indulge in a little mischief. I remember momma sitting under the dryer with curlers in her hair. My momma, being a school teacher, had that uncanny sense of what was going to happen before it happened, and could give you "the look" that you had better behave. Well, for some reason on this day I missed "the look". I was just trying to show how helpful I could be and ended up pouring a whole pan of curlers onto the floor! Momma was out from under that dryer quicker than you say "Jack Robinson", and I was automatically bawling my eyes out! I got a spanking right then and there. I didn't cry because I had made a mess or because Momma had spanked my hind end, which, yes, I needed. I was crying because I had disappointed her.

You have to understand, when I was growing up most kids had respect for their parents and did what their parents said. One didn't blatantly do what they wanted even though their parent had said not to do it, or to go and do something different. Respect seems to be elusive today.

Now, don't let my story confuse you. There is a difference between obeying and respecting. To obey someone means to comply with their request. Respect means to treat someone's feelings with importance. That isn't saying that their feelings are more important than yours but…. you care enough to place some sort of significance on how they feel.

Understand, even as a young child I was very compassionate and respectful, so, when I could see how embarrassed and upset my momma was with me for making a mess, it broke my heart. I was crying because I felt like, even though it was an accident, I had let her down, as well as the ladies working there, who had trusted me and was allowing me to play with the curlers.

Proverbs 22:6 says, "train a child up in the way they should go and when they get old they shall not depart from it." I am thankful to my parents for making sure I grew up respectful of others, having compassion for others, and being a strong, educated, independent woman.

Peace, Love, and Blessings!

Saving Myself

Try as you might, I will not break,
the walls are built too high.
To protect and save myself from feelings,
lest I die.

Your words, they cut like a knife,
But I don't feel the pain,
I am numb to all this strife and
I will not take the blame.

You so underestimate,
Listening to the spoken word,
Such a difference in hearing and listening
My speech, it isn't slurred.

You do not listen with intent to understand,
You should listen instead of speak.
Broken may be my heart,
but I am no longer weak.

Often we underestimate,
the silence of a listening ear,
It's overwhelming to consider
What words I may hear.

All being said and done
Your words burnt into my soul
I am now but one
And no longer under your control.

Self Acceptance

I manage to spend some swing time, occasionally, with my cousin. Sometimes it seems as if the swing time is way over due. I so love our talks, and even the brutal honesty we have with each other is so refreshing! Each time we talk, I end up realizing a new truth about life, or myself, as does he.

One day in particular, we both had a realization, from total different ends of the spectrum. What's so funny is, for me, today it actually hit home. I have been coming into a world of self acceptance over the past few months and today, it finally hit me. It finally smacked me up side the head and almost brought me to tears, and I had to step back, breathe, and wrap my head around a few things.

In nursing school, I remember writing a paper about how I was supposed to be feeling about things going on, and never really feeling them, just going through the motions that were expected. I guess that's how I always handle things.

Well, today I guess I realized that I am not as comfortable with myself as maybe I want to be or that I want people to think I am. I have made strides in this endeavor, but I am not where I yearn to be. You see, I am permanently flawed. Having this type of existence can be more than miserable. Living for the praise and respect from others will do nothing to quiet the voices in my head. These voices continually remind me that I am not quite good enough. Unfortunately, the voices are not all mine. They at times come from friends and family, in what I want to think of as loving and caring but tend to be more destructive at times, only because I allow it.

No one deserves my love and respect more than myself! Overcoming how I think about myself and accepting myself is a definite challenge. I have found that, just maybe, people accept me more than I accept myself. That is a dangerously sad realization. These feelings are more than overwhelming, they are somewhat intoxicating. Learning to celebrate who I am and accepting myself is an ongoing task. We are all sacred and magnificent beings. We all deserve respect and consideration, but if we do not provide it for ourselves, we will be lost forever. Aristotle was a great philosopher who knew that "knowing yourself is the beginning of all wisdom." And, thanks to a little cousin time, I think I am on the verge of some wisdom myself.

Peace Love and Blessings!

Shenanigans

Well, it is a beautiful Autumn day, and I am taking advantage of my swing. My sidekick, Cookie Eloise, is busy doing her thing so I am sitting here thinking about my many friends.

I have been blessed with the opportunity to reconnect with many old friend, after what seems to be an eternity, and make many new friends, over the past few years. I love it when we have time to hang out, talk and just have fun. My swing time seemed to be a topic of discussion with the group.

Let me explain...
First, if you are reading this, you know and understand my swing time, and know that I share my true swing time with a very select few. I love to use a straw when I am drinking at a restaurant. Whether it is blowing the paper off or making a long straw to reach the other end of the table, it's always fun. I have been known, yes at a restaurant, to make a long straw to reach the other end of the table. It's all in fun and for laughs.

Anyway, a friend of mine brought me a whole box of commercial straws this past weekend. It was awesome but I had to wait on just the right moment to use them. Finally, it happened!!! I was told I couldn't reach a drink at the end of the table from my chair. Challenge accepted. The table was about 4 feet long and I was about 2 feet from the end of the table, so....I opened my bag, pulled out approximately 10 straws and began putting them together end to end.

While I was creating my extra long straw, conversations ensued about how one of our friends use to be "snobby", although now you would never know it. They discussed quite intently, as I pretended to not pay attention, how I would never be able to get a drink and how I knew just the right number of straws to choose. Hahahaha... Well, long story cut short, I stood up and was able to drink with my extra long straw.

Well, that is only a small excerpt of the shenanigans that happen with my friends when we have a shindig. I guess what I want to say is that we all grow up but friends will always be friends. Never be surprised by those 30 year old friendships and how they bounce right back like it was yesterday. Always be willing to forgive, because people don't always realize how they are acting. Keep in touch with those who are important to you.

Peace, Love, and Blessings!

Small Town Living

Being from a small town is not exactly a bad thing, although it can have its' down sides. Back in "the good old days" everyone seemed to know everyone, and everyone got along (for the most part). It was like being part of a huge family, and all families have that one person or group of cousins that just like to misbehave.

A town of churches and where dreams can come true, to this day, reminds me of coal furnaces, clotheslines with laundry hanging out to dry, apple trees, frog ponds, riding in the back of a '74 Ford, bicycles built for two, and I could continue. It was nothing to be out on my bike, be several blocks from the house, and as long as you were home for dinner no one worried.

The town, like all small towns has its share of secret places, places only those from the town know about. Places where teens go to sneak and drink, smoke pot, mess around, or those places where you can go to sit alone and contemplate life. Places where you could go to sit with a best friend and tell all your secrets, wishes, and wants for life. The winding country roads and nostalgia is something people in other parts of our country yearn for.

This weekend brings back so many memories! It is what we call SHINDIG weekend. Everyone comes home and it's like a big family reunion. Saturday night is always dinner and a bonfire where there are lots of stories, laughs, reminiscing, and photos. I hope everyone has a safe and fun filled weekend!

Peace, Love and Blessings!

Silence

The silence is like
A deafening scream
Of despair and heartache
Not found only in dreams.

The love that was lost
Can never recaptured be
The feelings of contentment
Never again will I see.

For in this life
True love comes but once
And my life is half over
This I am in acceptance.

The silence is slowly becoming
A welcomed friend
No more screams do I hear
My heart is on the mend.

For in this life
As convoluted as it can be
Changes never stop
Yet life has changed me.

The Cell That Is My Mind

I close my eyes,
And allow the veil to surround me.
Every heartbeat is echoed
In my head, likened to the waves crashing in the sea.
Every breath subconsciously noticing the fragrance of life, ignoring the
past while perceiving the present.
My thoughts begin with an understanding,
That knowledge concludes with reason,
And that I must acquiesce.
An exaggerated sensitivity
That transports me to places unknown,
The silence of the outside,
Trying to melt my heart of stone.
The absence of all that is negative,
The calm, it will prevail,
Turn back the hands of time,
Remove me from this cell.

Thing Change

Have I ever mentioned just how much I enjoy coming outside and sitting in my swing? Cookie Eloise is usually out here with me, but this morning she is inside, still sleeping.

I know I shouldn't have done it but I played hooky from church this morning. I should have gone, especially because I have a LOT on my mind right now. So many changes going on in my life. Oh, they are all good changes and exciting changes but at times, very scary and overwhelming.

Things change, that is a given. You can't stop the future from coming. You can't relive the past. You must be committed to the changes in your life. You must be thoughtful. Changes are not easy. Letting life flow from one day to the next, taking it one day at a time is the only way to survive.

Walking down a new path is difficult to say the least. You cannot be afraid of change. Take control of what you can change. Don't worry over what you can't. Worry doesn't change things. It will not give you control over the situation but it can cause you much sorrow. I have heard people say it is easier to stay in the hell they know than to venture into something different. Did they ever think the reason it is hell is because they never looked ahead to see the magic, the hope that change can bring? I mean, would you rather fish in a pond that is stagnant or a pond with clear water?

Eckhart Tolle made a point when he said," Some changes look negative on the surface but you will soon realize that space is being created in your life for something new to emerge." Well, that isn't saying change can't be painful, especially when we aren't comfortable or if we don't understand the reason for the change. You can't prevent the change from happening. You have to be ever thoughtful and seek the positives in all things, and see just how your life changes. That will be a change for the better. Generally, you won't see the positive at first, but God has a way of revealing it to us eventually, in His time. You see, God has a plan for each of us. We tend to fight Him daily, because we try to be in control instead of letting Him be in control.

Well, like I said, lots of things on my mind. Forget about the past for it is something you can't change, don't worry about the future because you have no way of knowing what will happen. Take life one day at a time. Enjoy life.

Peace, Love, and Blessings!

Time

Things come to you not when you want them, but when you need them. When you ask God for His help and guidance, chances are, the answer won't come immediately. Don't read into things that happen. Don't manipulate what happens to the way you want them. Allow God to work in your life and lead you where you need to go. The path won't be smooth. There will be trials to endure, from which we learn. There will be pain to endure, from which we grow. God doesn't cause these things to happen. Just like with our children, we sometimes allow them to do things we know they shouldn't. How else will they learn, for they don't always listen. Our children know we are always there, and we love them. We are there to protect them. God loves you, He is your fortress. When you give up, He carries you through the darkness. He love you through all your mistakes and failures. He is waiting on you to let him do exactly what he promised he would do, provide you with your needs. What you need and what you want are totally different things, so make sure you can differentiate the two. Phillippians 4:19 says "And this same God who takes care of me will supply all your needs from His glorious riches, which have been given to us in Christ Jesus."

Peace, Love and Blessings!

Best Friends

Well, it has been a beautiful day! The sun has been shining in the blue skies with a few scattered, white, full clouds here and there, and a nice warm breeze. The best part of this evening is getting to have some swing time while Cookie Eloise sniffs her way into a new adventure.

Living in the same neighborhood I grew up in is wonderful, yet at times sad. Some of the neighbors have passed on or moved away, while others are still ever present, but older and somewhat more frail that I ever expected them to be.

The neighborhood that I live in is a quiet place, and we all look out for each other. I may be a bit of a work-a-holic, but I know they keep an eye out for me, as I do them, and we don't have to see each other every day to know we are a phone call away if needed.

Living in Georgia, which seems like a lifetime ago, wasn't quite as wonderful. Some of our neighbors were great, while others would turn their heads to keep from speaking. I'm not saying that doesn't happen here but…..

Anyway, the actual neighborhood I grew up in, is a small town which holds many special memories as well as a few I would love to forget. Just like in the big city, we had some awesome neighbors and some that weren't so great. My best friend, since the age of 5, lived a block away, and we are still the best of friends today.

No matter where I have lived, who I have met, friends I have made or the changes I have gone through, some things are as constant as the stars in the sky. Just because you can't see them for the clouds, doesn't mean they aren't there, just like a best friend.

Best friends are there through the good, the bad, and the ugly and they pick you up when you fall. You see, you should know that being best friends is quite effortless. Becoming best friends take time and those friendships are cultivated. They are crafted, shaped, and created. This effort must be focused, otherwise the friendship will not last forever.

My best friends can break my heart, make me mad, make me cry, and yet no matter what, when the going gets tough, they are there 100%. You see, true friendships will last forever, even when telling the truth, no matter how bitter and unbiased it may be.

Make sure to let your best friends know how much you love and appreciate them. Don't take those special people in your life for granted.

Peace, Love, and Blessings!

Things Always Work Out

After a long day at work, I just wanted to come home and sit in my swing, especially with few warm days left. Who would have though that would be at 11:45 pm? I guess if Cookie Eloise must go out, so must I.

As I sit here I have been thinking about a conversation I had with a friend of mine this week. If you are going to do something, give 100%. Never give up. Things will always work out in the end. That doesn't mean they will work out the way you want them to, but they will work out for the best.

You see, the happily ever after is not perfect. It isn't knowing what is going to happen or when it will happen. It is taking risks, being yourself, and making choices. What you must remember is not to be afraid. Every risk has a consequence, so make the choice you won't regret. There are no true right or wrong answers in this life. Things are going to happen. Everyone has those days when everything goes wrong, and there are those days when the world is almost perfect.

No matter what happens, don't take anything or anyone for granted. Enjoy the life you have for it can change in the blink of an eye. Opportunities are made, so don't be afraid to go after what you want in life. No matter how hard or how easy it is, remember that your decisions will work out 100% the way they are supposed to work out.

Peace, Love and Blessings!

Thoughts Racing Through My Head

Thoughts racing through my head today. Swing sitting is so mind provoking and relaxing! My sweet Cookie Eloise prefers to stay indoors with the air conditioning, spoiled dog ☺. Wonder how that happened?

Sometimes, in my mind, I allow myself to simply disappear. When I do, it's like I'm not here at all, like I simply don't exist and cannot be found. Sometimes the feelings are so overwhelming I can hardly think and my head just seems to drift off with visions, some fabulous and others devastating. These visions seem so real and so vivid it makes me wonder if they are real, if I am real, if life is real or are we just a dream.

Sometimes I want to get so lost that I could never be found, never make my way home, and somewhere, start over again. I'd like to find a cabin in the mountains or a secluded beach and allow my thoughts to disappear, knowing that when they are gone, I will disappear as well; and see who, if anyone, notices my departure.

Sometimes I wonder if disappearing would allow me to feel more peaceful and feel more like the demonstrative, loquacious me that I used to be. Sometimes I think I may not want to disappear but that I just want to be found. Not found by just anyone, but the right one.

Sometimes it all finally makes sense and you realize that wanting to disappear is the problem, not the resolve. Life is too short to hide or to have regrets. No one ever said life was easy, but make good choices and life will be worth it. Love those that love you and forget those that do you wrong. Know that everything happens for a reason, good or bad, and if it changes you, allow that change to happen. Desiderius Erasmus said, "if you give light, the darkness will disappear in itself". Don't become the darkness!

Peace, Love and Blessings!

Time Passes

It's been quite a while since I've sat here in my swing and written anything. It feels odd without having my partner in crime, Cookie Eloise, sniffing around for her next big adventure. Oh, she is fine, just not living here anymore. So many things in my life have changed this year and I must say it is very exciting! Some things I can talk about, others I'm not ready to share with the world yet.

Well, this year I turned 49 on my birthday. Where has the time gone? I remember being in elementary school and wishing I was in high school. I remember in high school, wishing I was in college. Then I couldn't wait to get out of college and be an adult and live my life. Well, here I am, an adult, and at times I wish I were younger again, but all things said and done, I am happy with my life.

I have experienced a lot and it has made me who I am. Would I change anything? Well if we could all go back in time and have the knowledge we have now, of course we would change things. But since we can't, grab a hold of the life you have and make the best out of it.

I guess what I am trying to say, in a round about way, is that every single day / year you are alive is a blessing. Things change, you can't stop that, and you will age, you can't stop that either. As you grow older, you seem to learn more. Youth is a time for happiness and growth. Adulthood is a time for spreading those wings and maturing. No matter what our age, we have that desire for more, to reach for the stars. Live life with no regrets and enjoy it. Always invest in yourself. Turn your possibilities into realities. I have enjoyed every year of my life, even those years that held some type of loss, for it helped me grow. Love the life you have and embrace the lessons you learn.

Peace, Love, and Blessings!

To Thine Own Self Be True

Such a beautiful and glorious day! I am so thankful for my thinking spot, my swing, my Cookie Eloise, who always makes me smile, and for the many blessing I have in this life.

The past year I have been doing a lot of thinking and reflecting on my past and making plans for my future. Some of my writings may seem redundant, but when struggling to find oneself and reconnect or reinvent one's live, sometimes repetition is necessary. This helps you to establish a good understanding, not only for one's self but for others.

I have learned many things about myself. There is one thing that stands out amongst them all, and that is "to thine own self be true" as said by Polonius in Hamlet. You see, nothing at all matters more than our own esteem. Standing up for our principles, not assimilating and doing what we believe, invokes positive ideas.

For several years now, my head has been filled with ghosts from the past that seem to have been eating away at my soul. I decided that I can no longer allow this to happen day in and day out. Whether it is work related or personal, the subtle changes, that few have picked up on over the past year, are getting ready to become much more noticeable, for I am tired.

Now don't jump off the deep end. I am not changing who I am or who I am meant to be, just the way I allow myself to be treated and seen, not only by others but by myself.

Taking a long hard look at oneself can be a hard job and very time consuming. But, deciding to be honest and treat oneself with the respect and consideration one deserves can be just as difficult. What I have learned is that if you don't have those things for yourself, no one else will have them for you. Love yourself! To thine own self be true!

Peace, Love, and Blessings!

Fall

Sunday morning and I am sitting outside in my swing listening to the peaceful sounds of nature. The birds are chirping and there is minimal traffic to disrupt the peacefulness. Cookie Eloise is sitting on the sidewalk sniffing and guarding me and her home.

Autumn is such a wonderful time of year, although for many it brings sadness and depression. I prefer to feel the electricity in the air, smell the scent of the ripened earth ready to be harvested, and bask in the trees set a blaze with color just before they sleep for winter. Such magnificence and peace should not go without notice.

I think life should be perceived as the changing of the seasons. Look at the beauty each season has to offer. Seize the blessings you are provided. Respect the changes and grow with them. Know that each season comes with its own story and history. These stories and histories are very individual, very unique.

Every season has a purpose as does every season of life. Birth, cleansing, renewal, and death are all parts of life. Each season with its specific purpose and lessons to be learned. These help us to grow and mature like the trees. Once the lessons are learned, a new lesson is brought forth and seen like the age rings on a tree. One must welcome with open arms every predictable, commonplace, exciting, new, sensual, dying moment in this divine and sacred life we live. Respect each season as it is offered as a blessing.

Ernest Hemmingway, one of my favorites, said it best, "You're expected to be sad in the fall. Part of you died each year when the leaves fell from the trees and their branches were bare against the wind and the cold wintery light. But you knew there would always be the Spring, as you knew the river would flow again after it was frozen. "I think that allowing ourselves to revel in the metamorphosis is important. You have to find your own personal bliss. See life from within your soul and grab a hold of what you desire.

Live in faith that the seasons change. The beauty of each season will be proclaimed by you as your own seasons change and pass. Always look forward to the next season as a great adventure. Look with enthusiasm and optimism.

Peace, Love and Blessings!

Caught in the Net

The sound of the sea
Washes through my soul,
Cleansing my mind
Repairing the hearts hole.

The waves break
Reminding me of the pain,
As the waters flow
The feelings I try to explain.

The indifference of the sea
Engraved upon my heart,
Destruction of life
Revealed by this black heart.

The waters run deep
Trying to wash away the pain
But caught in a net
Feeling tied to a chain.

Unable to let go
Feeling devastated,
The abyss I am in
Barely is tolerated.

Life is so different
When you're broken and scared,
Always asking the question
"Why was my heart not spared?"

Yet the sound of the sea
Can nourish the soul,
Spawn life anew
Make my heart again whole.

Change Can Be Good

I woke up this morning thinking about my life in general. So many changes have happened the last few years. Both of my children have graduated from high school and college, divorce, job changes, death of family and friends and the list could go on. I am in a season of new beginnings. This time in my life is a new beginning and at times very overwhelming.

I am thankful to God that He is in control and has given me the peace and courage to start new and accept the changes with a smidgen of dignity and grace, for remember I am only human.

Sometimes it is hard to see the silver lining when the circumstances seem so devastating. Knowing there is a larger plan and that all things work for good for those who love the Lord truly brings about sense of freedom and calmness one could otherwise never understand.

There have been times I have prayed I wouldn't wake up the next morning and there have been times I have ask, "what the hell, God?" But, I know that no matter what anyone on this earth thinks of me or tries to do to me, God is the man with the plan. Look at what He did for all of us!

I guess what I really want to say is that change, as hard as it can be at times, is good, especially when you allow yourself to see the big picture. The things you go through only allow you to find your true self and only YOU know who you really are.

Just a quick thought process for another day. It can't be too bad, I was allowed to wake up this morning so it is definitely a blessed day. Keep things in perspective, stay positive, and remember how blessed you are!

Peace, Love, and Blessings!

Christmas Poetry

Was the day before Christmas while at work I did spy, 8 tiny reindeer and sleigh in the sky. "Ho ho ho, Merry Christmas", to the man I did say; then I ask "are you stopping at my house today?" You're getting nothing, for you have been bad... this comment cut to the bone and it made me sad. But then I thought of Jesus our Savior, who was born on this day in a tiny manger. In a town named Bethlehem so far away from the Christmas that we celebrate today. Jesus is Lord and his gift to me, is more than I could ever ask for, you see. He was born of the Virgin Mary and raised as a man, he died for my sins, part of a greater plan. He's made the deaf to hear and the blind to see, the mute to speak and he saved you and me.

Peace, Love, and Blessings!

A Place Where You Can Connect

I was outside alone early this morning sitting in my swing, when the rain started pouring and then I noticed the lightening and began to hear the thunder in the distance. No, I didn't rush inside, because my swing is covered, but I was sitting there thinking about life in general. Thinking about what the day may hold, what tomorrow will bring and how I can make an impact. Proverbs 27:1 says… "Do not boast about tomorrow, for you do not now what a day may bring."

One thing I do know, each day is special, a learning experience, and your own personal cherished place where you can ground yourself and find yourself when your feeling lost or unsettled is one of those important things in life. Whether it is a swing, top of the mountain, the beach or wherever, we all have that one special place where we can connect with out feelings and concentrate on whatever it is we feel we need to think about.

I hope each of you find your special place. I want you to find the peace and happiness life has to offer. Understand, the little things in life are just as important as the big ones, for they are the groundwork for our tomorrows, and none of us want a poor foundation.

Peace, Love, and Blessings!

The Story of My Calling

My grandmother and mother were both school teachers, along with several great aunts and great uncles. I remember growing up and playing school with my grandmother very often. When my cousins would come visit, we would play school, with Mamaw being the teacher, and us being the students. When they were not there, Mamaw and I would still play school. We would use the pictures of my cousins as other students. She would call on me to answer questions or she would call on one of them, pretending they were giving her the occasional correct answer. Of course, when they gave the wrong answer she called on me for the answer. If I answered incorrectly, she of course as one of their pictures and would repeat the correct answer they gave. This helped me to determine that I wanted to teach when I grew up. I wanted to help people learn things like she did. I wanted to be a teacher! But remember I said I wanted to help people.

As Mamaw aged, Momma had take more time with her and she would have to do things for her. I didn't mind helping Momma take care of Mamaw at all. It was during this time that my mother saw something in me that I did not realize, and she began pushing me to think about the nursing field.

You see, although my mother was well aware of my calling to be a nurse, it was something that I was not aware of until a little later on in life. Actually, until after I had been a nurse for several years, I did not realize how I loved taking care of people. It was my passion. It was that passion that aligned itself with my belief systems and it made me feel as if I truly made a difference. The best part was that I got to teach people, so in essence, I did become a teacher. In some ways, the dream to be a teacher was achieved.

I did not realize until about five years ago that there was still a hunger in me that needed to be ignited. I had always played around with writing poetry and silly things through the years. My first year in college, many years ago, I realized that I enjoyed writing papers and coming up with short stories. That may have been when I first realized my love for writing. Who would ever have thought that a paper on the large cockroaches at the beach would spark my interest in writing?

Since my unfortunate divorce, and I say unfortunate because I always expected the happily ever after, I have had much time to think and write. I have written from my heart with such overwhelming angst at times to astounding happiness at others. My mother died before I could graduate from nursing school. My father is still alive and retired from the railroad. Through the past few years, I have learned that I am very much an individual. I have been learning to love myself and not worry about anyone else's judgment, for they should not be judging me in the first place. Learning to not care what other think has been a struggle for me. It isn't that I don't care about their opinions, especially those of my father, but I am learning to respect my own decisions. You see, focusing on my decisions and my goals help to keep me looking ahead. This way I don't keep looking behind me wondering what if I had done this or that. I have read that there is no amount of guilt that can change the past. I guess that means there is no amount of anxiety that can stop the future.

I am a strong person and I have learned that strong people haven't had an easy past. They work hard and have been through more than you can realize. Their life has many chapters, as does mine, and I can only hope mine will have many more. I don't compare any other person's journey with mine. One thing that I have learned about my calling is that it is never to late to be who or what you want to be. I love writing and want my writings to be inspirational to others. Being afraid of change or afraid to allow myself to evolve is not an option. Stepping onto a new path is very scary and difficult, to say the least. One thing I have learned is that I must be loyal to myself. This loyalty is what has allowed me to grow and change. It has been a challenge and has also allowed me to realize who I am and understand what I think. One's thoughts determine what they believe is possible. If you are expecting positive, you will see positive. So, I have learned to speak it as if it is so.

My calling to write has sent me on a journey I never could have imagined. It is an extraordinary event that I hope will inspire others to chase their dreams. My nursing career, which I love, has taught me so much more than I could have ever imagined. Thanks be to God for his guidance and love, for without Him, I would not be where I am today.

Edwards Brothers Malloy
Thorofare, NJ USA
October 5, 2016